Moms Are The Strongest Men

Moms Are The Strongest Men

Raquel Medora

MOMS ARE THE STRONGEST MEN

Cover art by Nanalee Nichols

ISBN: 979-8-218-62890-1

Table of Contents

Section I

losing it

i look for the lost slipper
under the pile of clothes
dumped out in pieces
of pajama tops and one-piece
swimmies

the black slipper with one strap
to tie down those wiggly-
piggly toes

the slipper lost last september

i fold the clothes in piles
of pjs and shorts and t-shirts
i look for the blue shirt to match
the new pajama bottoms

lost in the bottom of a bottomless chore
in the sewn seams of cotton undies
i see the train tracks from a lost dream
tracing a feeling

like floating in water
watching fall colors cover the hills
pulling fog over the tops of their heads
remembering to ask for a sip of coffee

as steam pours out over my knuckles
off the tip of the train

i pour into the sand
i see the tops of the grand canyon
and hike my way back
as friends call down to me

below, echoes etched into the fur
of a grey and hungry coyote
my feet trace the path back to the top

orange dust, hazy and fading
like i lost someone along the way

c-section medley

open incision

indecision

i did not say yes

holding a mask over my mouth

breathe, breathe, breathe

the oxygen for the life inside me

six nurses rush in

bark orders

monitors cords catheters tubes

in motion in the air

connected to me

my entourage roll me out

sling me into a door

my mouth silenced

by inhales

exhales into an empty mask

which o.r.? which o.r.?

room selected at random

the six file in,

on-call doctor

regrettably

introducing herself
anesthesia upped the antics

i can't feel my feet

the doctor listing numbers
and letters in sequences
like morse code for my belly
slice open and push firmly
a gush of warm fluid spilling out
of me onto my numb tummy
i thought i heard the first signs of life
gurgling from gouging out part of me
and moving my insides into shambles
a weight finally lifted
then another

i hear her angelic voice
a sweet, feminine, lullaby

i look at her purple body

and look away quickly
my dry mouth bothers me
my shaking body
convulsing
uncontrollably
my impatience to sit up
so i could breathe
like living under water without gills
without hands to hold my baby
my body fluid as if nothing
is holding me together

in dreams

i open my eyes
with my arms still squeezing
the pillow tight
right in front of me
dreaming of holding
my baby i gasp
thinking i've hugged her too tight
feeling light
too light
then her crying
from the other room
scares me back to life

phantom kicks

gaseous knocks on my stomach walls
like baby hands tapping inside me
but i'm deflated now
the tremor of movement
in a split second
reminiscent of months past
when we were attached

you cry to be tapped on the back
i cry to be alone

tapping keys

I find that it's obvious,
the decay, the hardening
lines on the skin that begins to thin.

I picture a muffin,
round and plump and soft,
sweet like a fig right from the tree.

I fall on the cracked concrete,
look down at my busted knee -
all you see is bust, not me.

I ask for reprieve. I ask -
I feel like a burning tree.
Cracking branches
hooked under, like waving hello,
trying not to let go,
break,
while you scream at your kids
climbing the ashy branches
too high

what weight would it take?

I think the weight is too heavy.

I think it's too hard to carry.

I think it's better I'm not a
burning tree, but

I'm still a mommy.

deciphering your cry

i.

5:50 in the morning
      in the morning
so late it's early
      and late
whining and crying   <screaming>
then crying and whining

i lie and wait
unable to move
      but my body is unnerved
the blood shakes in my veins
and defers a depression-like-state
into   motion

ii.

he's slapping my chest

and flopping

and crying

and whining

and crying

and whining

have you ever wondered
at 5 am
who else is awake?

iii.

sucking and crying

my body hunched

    trochoidal shape

he's pinching my skin with baby talons
gripping my skin

    to become one skin again

iv.

i cry and whine and whine and cry
my skin droops
the milk has made it thin

i want to sleep on a bed in a treehouse in the lush costa rican
rainforest
hear the howler monkeys
and the pitter-pattering rain

V.

i sit on the toilet

the howling toddler comes crashing
into so many things

grabbing the wooden step-stool
dropping it on the floor
grabbing it
and knocking it into the cabinets -
the closet door

getting a bandaid
asking me to open it

griping at me
for trying to put it on her

- she puts it on - yelling *chadwick*

ten times

chasing chadwick
with a toddler-sized shopping cart
filled with bags of chips
falling onto the floor
with each aggressive turn
she takes

vi.

did i make a mistake?
i'm always making mistakes
i'm writing instead of playing
i'm writing instead of listening
i'm writing instead of crying
i'm writing instead of screaming
i want to hold them in my arms forever
and i want my freedom again
to hold myself
warmly
and kindly

regret:

re•gret: (v.) /rəˈgret/

when you don't trust that your past self made the best decision at the time to best meet your needs. This is a repercussion of having hindsight. However, your past self was meeting the needs of that present moment, not your future self, who now feels the consequences. Regret can be a side effect from grief.

She regretted getting married, shackled almost eternally by an institution shameful enough on which to blame. She regretted curling her hair as the weather became untamed. She regretted not smiling more, but she couldn't help the rage.

tantrums

when she kicks her feet so hard
the toilet bowl might crack in two
and unleash the turd precariously floating below

unwilling to accept the help of an elder,
more practiced diarrhea-wiper,
she frantically grabs toilet paper and yells
NOOOO
pushing the elder away to put her index finger
right
in the
pooh.
the elder yells
FINE DO IT YOURSELF!
WASH
YOUR
HANDS
and storms off
in a flare of panic
because she caught
the terrible-twos

later on instagram
some expert in child-rearing
provides calm, practiced tips
for toddler tantrums
and the elder sighs

isn't it obvious?

inundating mothers
with tips
on having grace
for their children
without first
providing grace
for the mothers
is only going to cause the mother to throw her phone across
the room

resulting in a shattered family heirloom,
obviously

helicopter hen

in and out and back again,
swinging from the arm of a tree,
as a toddler,
playful and free,
the leaves shake and rustle,

fussing over the curls in her baby's hair,
hens lying down on their feathered beds,
ruffling and shaking,
bocking and squawking,
beady eyes twitching
while looking at the world
they can't seem to see

Green-Eyed Momster

It's true that the green-eyed momster has glowing green eyes that are lit by the light of the long, grueling day, from maintaining homeostasis at home, filtering emotions and ugly thoughts of sticky floors, sticking dirt to the bottom of her barefoot pores. It's true she grows aglow when the moon appears and she keeps hearing no and the whiny pleads from a toddler that has pled all day. And when the eyes glow green she becomes mean. She barks and shouts and gets on the ground, grabs and grunts as she puts her children back to sleep. Momster is green, bleeding desire to be seen, but her efforts are what they are: expected. She runs out the room to howl at the moon and slips on the spoon she grabbed before noon when she was going to eat but had to feed them each different things and then put up dishes and started laundry and picked up toys and played and bathed and somehow got one to sleep. But now her feet are in pain and her feelings aren't the same with the bluest of violets hung up above her bed to dry as she cries before sleep because both eyes are open, waiting to hear either child's feet or a moan. Now she closes her bright green eyes and sleeps, but ever so lightly because the glow is so unnerving.

Section II

What is the purpose of Woman?

Does she cook?

Does she clean?

Does she take her child to school?

Does she feed them?

Does she feed me?

Does she feed all of society?

Does Woman gratify our pleasures?

Is she nice?

Is she clean?

Does she fit into our box we locked with a key?

Is she straight?

Is she gay?

How old is she today?

Will she wash the blood from our hands?

Will she kiss them and pleasure us?

How many times will we hurt her?

Will she forgive us?

She is Woman.

She carries the world in her womb.

Do we care for her then?

Do we care for her children?

Do we care for her without children?
Do we care for her worldly womb?
Do we dare care for her mind?
Does she think?
Does she feel?
Who is this Woman?
Is she smart?
Does she obey?
Okay, then she can have her career one day,
with conditions.
What's her value?
How much is she worth?
Will she come home if she's worth more?
How many kids will she have?
Is she looking old?
But she's still virtuous, she has her home and children and
chores and of course, her underpaid work. She'll see our
worth. She won't leave.
She is Woman.
Will she turn society's wheels a bit longer?
Will she nurse us back to health now?

Woman, where are you? You have more work to do.
Please.

Breast Obsessed

look at those milky jugs
bounce as she runs out of town
followed by the hound
watched all around
sweat and milk drip from her
and they still can't seem to catch her
she bends, then aches
her baby on her hip sways
she shakes hands like a man
and mows and weed-eats
shops and re-seeds
she multi-tasks
and if you ask
she might want you to stay
sweep and fold
until her list fades
she browses
wondering about love
could she accept the care of a lover
if they appeared today
would she want the love of a man

or the tenderness of a woman
to fill her cup with breasts
nursing herself back to good health
she decides
Goddesses are far more fulfilling

engorgement

gravity yanks at the skin under my eyes
i grow wings out of my back
at first the pain
a dull, subtle note
as thick white feathers form
and protrude from the center
of my upper spine
then my shoulder blades begin to ache
where the wings have now separated
the arches take shape
to unveil thick
white, feathery humps
the first flight is the shakiest
white feathers dripping from the sky
and as i fly
the pains become a cadence of back aching
but i continue to glide
fluidly rising
along the currents
in the night sky

Organic Milk

whose feelings matter more
i want to feed my son
i don't think twice
in a place with women
with other children - babies -
but i'm told
don't do that here
another parent may see you
a dad may see you
he may be bothered
as if the space i take
with my son
in one room
versus the other
one side
or the other
provided more comfort
more safety
for the others
as if to say
i'd rather hurt you

your feelings
and shame you
and make you think twice
than hear what another parent has to say

as if i would have remained silent
as if my confidence and comfort
within myself and motherhood
bothered them
made them feel out of place

without shame
can i just be mom
not working mom
not stay at home mom
not baby mama
not single mom
not milf
not tired mom
Mom

observations

you try to grab the pen-point-sized-scab
on the top of my foot
drool rolling off my pinky toe
pointer finger touching a freckle on my ankle
like a crumb on the floor
inspecting the composition of me

i am not comprised of shame
i am not comprised of grief
i am not comprised of fear or anxiety
i am comprised of cells
your small, two-inch-long pointer finger is cells
we hold energy within these cells

they take up space
like the freckled artwork on our skins
a mecca of landscape

in my heart

i see the blue
beads that interlock
and mock my hidden
hurt and fate
buh-boom
she said
from the miniature
rocking chair
a remark to mock
the wooden trellises
in my body's orbit
frequently fiendish
and impoverished
by Love
trying to cope
knowing love
is saved for those
most willing
to open
to hurt
to ask

to demand
do i fit
the silly little bill?

the joys of childrearing

incomparable as much as it is unbearable
and insatiable
the love nestled in my bones
caressing the veins that have harbored
the overpumping of past traumas
there's no bouncing back
or looking back
or pretending my body didn't transform
to harbor your own hearts and blood and love
as much blood lost my blood gained
and changed
in having you each transform me
i must set perfection and standards and fears aside
to love you both to love parenthood wholly
you both came from my heart
after all

v is for virgo

if i wrote you a memoir of the last 365 days
there would be fleeting moments of static, warm days
sitting on the bed, watching the light from the sunset fade
feeding hungry bellies and drowning in other people's
stories
waking up tired and wanting
water in a plastic cup, lukewarm from sitting on the counter
all day
and water rushing, rushing to make it to the ocean just in
time
panicking that the great day would be missed
water mixing with water and spraying rainbows on the
horizon's sky
baby toes and runny noses and packed-lunch-fridays
moving furniture and vacuuming and scrubbing plates
the hand-me-down high-chair desecrated...
sticky floors, oh, the sticky floor woes!
dust and hair and dirt
play and new friends, kneeling on the dog-scent-stained
carpets
water gun fights and standing up for women's rights

missing socks and forgetting meetings and milk on
packed-lunch-fridays
missing home and tiny hands pulling my hair
laughing with friends on sundays and being wine drunk at a
hotel bar on a monday
letting people help me and love me and listen to me
ear infections and fevers, loneliness creeping
crying in front of teachers over breastfeeding
crying over unkind words and overworking
pursing lips to quiet the tears from seeping out in waiting
rooms and offices
you wouldn't believe the ways the days have pulled me
stretching every fiber of my being to fit all that life in this
precious, small space

Section III

i'm cold now

i'll say one day when all the hairs on my pretty little head go
gray
as the strands metamorphosize from warm to cold from
yellow to white like a dim light notched up on the dimmer
enlightened by years sun-filled and the darkest of hours
butter that was once softened put in the fridge to harden
and decay no longer a fruitful garden here where the strands
evolve from soft
to coarse and gray, obstinate strands unwilling to slither into
your hands not puddy not dough just rough, crooked, stiff
hands that have unearthed and planted and held and
coddled and written and typed and stroked and waved and
grabbed and shook and punched and drove and played and
caressed and saluted
holding hands
one foot in the grave with the fits over grays and whites but
it's the softest, slowest, smoothest wish to move into
whiteness subtly, slowly, kindly
hold yourself,

hold space, embrace aging with grace

prolific

we are bound like warm leather straps
holding together the soft pages of a story
that disappears after it's told

the smell of a baby like warm milky pudding
hands cupped around his face
to self-soothe when he's irate:
teeming-tyranny-total-meltdown
food-throwing, throbbing hearts

hands holding glowing growing green
with wanting to be heard
felt
understood

seen

i'm a prickly pear

pink and floral
round and sharp
i'd like to poke you
make you bleed
i bleed
rub off the waxy seed
you'll see
mix me in a margarita
grill me
watch me burn
they'll ask
how was *she*

i sit on the desert slope
there are lots of me
but none exactly like me
and i grow
alone
watching the coyotes pass
the deer lifting their heads
to listen

the oaks wilting
the slope changing from grass to homes
birds and their chirping
the sky dusty with pollen
and maybe i'll live
a prickly life forever - quietly

solitude

the wind chimes still sing
even without an anchor
the vent on the house flaps shut
as wind brings the dry,
cool, fall air
in painful inhales

breathe

i am not surprised

mama bears protect her cubs from their fathers
who might eat them alive for dinner with a beer.

orangutan moms can't put down their babies
while they build their thousand homes and turn the
pancakes on the stove.

cheetah moms pack the van with the cubs and sporadically
uproot to keep the babies safe, creating inseparable sibling
bonds over their mother's flippant choices in rv parks.

elephant grandmothers will take their granddaughters in
from college and say they need to put some more meat on
their bones with a little nudge of a tusk and wink of an ear.

must everything in my life be poetic

a black balloon shaped like a fat star floats up from a house

it's shadow passes along the sidewalk

startlingly dark and heavy for something empty

plastic covered couches

have such meaning

the suffocated cushions

the emblem of American culture

plastic covered couches

plastic bag over a child's face

plastic covered couches

plastic ziplocs over sandwiches, chips, and grapes

plastic covered couches

plastic covered couches

plastic covered couches

Yellow

sunflowers with metal leaves and pecan trees line the main street. rusted rooftops reflecting light like life's peak. malbec in a corner like sugar running down a hummingbird's throat. in my garden rocks and paper cut leaves and feet for thorns and heated lamps like baby hugs. crying fires dripping down from sunkissed petal skin. summer solstice surging sewage-politics and barrels of guns running from rum and paper-pay-less shops. american elm and hooves for feet cactus on the street trotting past pecan pieces and decades of skull feces. sunflowers, run flowers, rum flowers, yellow and burgundy money.

summer evening

you know when it's 8pm
and the air is still warm
fulfilled by the long, tight hug
from the sun
and you open the front door
the wall of buzzing
shimmying into your ears
and you grab the water hose
when you turn it on
the rubber
having been hot all day
and the water
spouting out
like your first drink of water
the smell isn't quite metallic
but thick and green
warm to the touch
like if a sunflower had blood in its veins
you hear the water
eager to reach the life
thirsty for her nourishment

the point

rolling up like this- bun up, pimple on my brow
furrowed and ruffled
curls untamed
nipples protruding 'cause
fuck the patriarchy
livin' on a split-six-hour-sleep
nursing and feeding
chasing like chirping birds needing

describe the sleepless pain
is it wakefulness in a dream-like-state?
stagnant, algae bloom lakes
putrid and boiling hot in my birth month's boiling vain?
i wake like -

beep. boop.
craving,
denied the shit that helps keep people sane

blow some more hot wind in my face

before the heat rolls in, thick and moist

sit under the pubescent green leaves
leave me lying under the trees

death and sleeplessness
parenting and umbilical cords
coffins and rituals

open your sleepy eyes
you'll see

ancient remedies

can you tell me?
how the roots
and the leaves
listen
while I place my hand
on their trunks
and ask them
to whisper their wisdom
as if the bark could bark
orders at me
about how to save a marriage
how to serve
how to hide emotions
in a vaulted reserve
how the calluses on my memories
have lived in my brain in vain
can it snap back into place
as if snapping wouldn't just break
a branch away

without a roof
the air is like transparency
voiceless and present
no facet of truth to unearth
your hands like wiggling worms
ambition like a slippery snail
hidden face of a temptress
let her, like water, wash away

summer opens

her mouth cracks

                    a dirty, crooked alligator grin
            asphalt grips as tires
ride the edge of man and earth
                i hear her voice in the night
        again
                    greyed out under the
            rumble
        of another plane
i whisper to myself a list
      printing company printer
                books letters
                  cafes bookstores
          creating a fine line
to cross and begin to race the tracks

        like the rainbow bridge
     to the end
somewhere in the abyss

Section IV

Opening My Mouth to Find I Can't Speak

Have you had one of those dreams? One where you need to scream but your mouth opens and you find that nothing is released; no air, no grunts, no growls, absolutely nothing, like a dead person who can't intervene when their words are in question now?

As if this dream is reminding you of your own reality, one where your voice is nothing in comparison to the giant floating rock with billions of living people who speak and trillions long gone who spoke, of which, only a handful whose words were worth re-speaking.

And this isn't even the tea. This isn't even the real reason you find you can't speak because your dream-state-brain does not ponder the masses so widely in such a dream. Your dream-state-brain is still thinking, "what about me?" It is upon waking that you see, the noise you create has entered into a void because of the people who aren't listening.

Dear Men in Power

Sit while I zip your mouth shut
like your loose-lipped-pant-zipper
stuck on a bare nut
after you were dared to fuck the assistant up the elevator,

your hand the escalator,
her shoe stuck,
her body puddy,
glued to the wall with a sticky fear.

Sit while I speak you into a woman's frame,
the second you have sex
the terror of God shivering through your veins
preparing your vessel to grow life for life to be born in vain.

Sit while I grab the back of your throat
while my other hand pulverizes your pea brain -

a single woman at a bar,
targeted and eyed, walking home just before night,
grabbed and thrown into a van;

when the door shuts, it decapitates her from speaking again.

Sit and hear the cries of every silenced mouth you've spoken
over,
demeaned with silly words that mean absolutely nothing in
the grand scheme of things,
but have smeared this woman's brains into thinking she
could never compete.

Sit and hear the words I will fuck sideways into your brains,
"You mean nothing,
you are nothing,
you exist as nothing...
without a mother,"

as the mother hangs off like a low sigh,
breathing heavily into your ear,
caressing the hairs on your neck to remind you of the cries of
pain that sing in your spine from the divine womb from
which you came.

Sit for a minute as I grab the last laugh from the jar of candy.

Sit while I grab the coffee pot's last cup.

Sit as I peer through the door you forgot to keep shut.

Sit and shut the fuck up for once.

"There's no Such Thing as the Gender Pay Gap,"

said a man.

9 out of 10 researchers agreed that men thought differently
than women:

they were more sexual, more aggressive, more ambitious,
more logical, and of course, smarter.

9 out of 10 researchers were men.

9 out of 10 researchers graduated with a Bachelor of Science
degree.

9 out of 10 researchers felt superior to their colleagues.

9 out of 10 researchers died from heart disease.

1 out of 10 researchers fell from the sky.

mother origin

pi•ous: (adj.) /ˈpīəs/
oftentimes associated with someone (fem.) who possesses good-naturedness, but is in direct correlation to their need to fulfill religious obligations. Someone who is good, is pious.

She is a pious woman. She does not curse. She does not drink. She goes to church twice a week. She is wholesome. She is without negativity. We love her for her piousness.

We love her for her motherly love. We love her for her kindness. She thinks of others incessantly. Women should be selfless. Women should be home. Women should be shy and quiet and obedient. Women should be *pious*.

we Evolve

sometimes
we move forward
with time when we break
like bread the cyclical
trauma roaming around in
our heads
imparting body shaming comments
into our veins
and asking us to carry
this all too heavy weight

| boxes |

incomplete moving / new cities / faces to put in / boxes
that have never seen the light of day

say black boxes / or white boxes / or cold boxes / or warm
boxes / you can't put your curling iron in the bathroom box
and the beauty box / but the faces / are round / the bodies
are shaped like /\ trees and boxes \ can't be without their
mother trees

your clothing box labeled | neat-freak |
your kitchen box labeled | ADHD |

your luggage stuffed with stuffed toys you kept so many you
don't have names for all of them / your scarves shoved into a
small box / with a small label / you printed and thought
about mailing to the last / mansplainer \ that wanted to call
your number \ but instead called you *dumb*

then when you tape them all up / pack them in the moving
truck / and still have cleaning supplies / to stuff in the back
of your Ford named | Ninny |

you forgot the crate / the one with your | PTSD &
generalized anxiety |

time, time, time, time's passage / restores the conveyor belt...
that carries your crate across the continent and finds you
hunched over in the corner of your new apartment on |
Nameless Street | and you cry because you can't unpack the
clutter the world has been naming for | you |

Thought Exercise: Think of Something Weird and Ambiguous

You might think about the space between your toes or the time between high school and college or meeting a new friend in a bar where you felt completely out of place.

You might think about the time you lived without taking breaths in your mother's womb and the muffled hums and drums of her existence putting you to sleep.

I think about the energy we all possess and how it's both free and enslaved. Emotions coming and going as they please and our bodies encapsulating all that moves freely within.

I think about the confines of labels and being told who to be and how to act. I think about the years I've spent wanting normal: to be normal, to feel normal. And the defiance that comes with being weird and different.

I think about how weird it is to be an artist with a corporate job, living in a consumerist society.

I think about consumerism that tries to sell you on your own individuality and style, while simultaneously congregating you with the masses.

Now tell me that's not weirder than a foot fetish. At the very least, it's far more confusing.

i hate this fucking state

when they went *ooh, ahh* finding
bible verses and beliefs so clever
they signed the Declaration of [Eternal Slavery]
with a conviction so strong, Jesus looked atheist.
quills wet like the blood and sweat
a steadying hand
posh, deserving, above all else
smoking tobacc'er on a wooden porch
a creaky rocker like the creaky slave - person - woman -
mother - wait
watch me slingshot their hate
across the face
of this god-forsaken state

Womanly Love

I want to hit so hard your face goes sideways. I want to run so fast the sky swallows me whole. I want to hold you down like the earth's core. I want to pave the way like a steamroller. I want to crack your bones with one handshake. I see you shake when I say your name. I crumble every man's last name a woman had to embrace. I breathe a fire that ignites change. Watch me. Watch me. Watch me. Watch me.

Sorry Professor, I'm Writing Another Political Poem

in pain, united we stand
marching to be shot
bullets
or tear gas
tear us apart
rioting on the walk
for rape and rape rights
3 white men
vote
and we scream
a resounding *NO*
signatures snaking
like raping the ground
unearthing our mothers' mothers' mothers' mothers
money trails
to your pockets
from mine to yours
and you claim me as yours
my birthrights you keep fucking
oh, your money shot's coming

bubbling over

tea kettle whistling
or covid wheezing
or kneeling over to kiss
this toddler-dirty ground
grown from the cells
that kept us captive
i'm not sure which came first
but i know it was woman
throw a fit - ok - my cares
got left in the mail too long
with that pair of keys and your
voter registration card after moving
toll bills nothing like a tolling bell
fists in a bucket
grinding ice cream
missing weekends
missing meetings and notes left - be back by tuesday -
a cursed country
passions bleeding
heed warning - worry,
your money-tummy is needing feeding

Section V

Baby Blue Beluga Blowhole

Again, it's lodged in the back of my throat, thick like the air about to blow from the hole on the top of a baby beluga whale. But I smile, while I'm drowning. I fell asleep in the ocean, standing on the treasure ship I call home. The view thick with microbes floating around me. My treasure box empty. Instead of diamonds, it's filled with plastic rings from candy wrappers and rocks I found in Little Rock.

The mast alone and angled, straight as my back that aches when I wake from sleeping 8 hours straight. Another day. The lull of the water is as loud as silence. A breathing, while breathing, for me, is not allowed in the deep blue sea. Humming, washing the babies' clothes again and again. Brush your teeth. Wash your hands. Brush your teeth before you sleep.

Woman without bars

scary, terrifying
you're audibly shaking
she's fluid
undefined
does as she pleases
cares not for you
or your caresses of shame
your verbal slashes
backlashes
impounded by your laughter
you're audibly shaking
i hear your boots
wet feet
where you peed
watching her stand on two feet
when you couldn't contain her
couldn't tame her
couldn't beckon her to your feet
what the energy
what the ever-loving hell
who is She?

Rocky, the Rat Killer

i can't un-smell the dead rat
on my walk back home
wafting to my nose
while i waited for toddler toes
to turn back home
away from the rotting rodent

then i ran over a rat
while driving up the driveway
flat with tendrils
dragged across the concrete
into the garage
god this shit stinks

i scraped its massacred body

into the bush next to the garage

this is the third rat this week

two others dead in my garden
from whatever witch's brew spices
had spells already cast to kill
pesky creatures like these

the whole family is probably mourning
holding three funerals over their poisoned
and flattened sons in one week

too many young rats die this way
victim to women like me

rolling wave

wispy curls clicking the sides of my face {whip whip}
steamroll and ramble lull and empty the burden of buckets
unturned sitting in a pile under the clicking lights third floor
apartment hallway the smells of an unsettled earthworm
wiggling and wobbling rolling worms down the driveway
crisp with the sun's tempting licks departure by the curve
running to wave seeing sadness on her face
goodbye goodbye -
an abbreviated love

coil in the soil you little slinky snake

black kettle

keep the secret
tucked under my tummy
touch the floor
tipped over to pull pigtails
tangled ends out
the slamming backdoor
toppling toddlers
onto sticks and tricks and toads
and trips to the pond
sinking stones that
skipped so close
torrent tricks and
trembling water tipping
off the clogging log
timer ringing
unclogging the drains
opening gates and lifting
a tent between
the sectional and
the ottoman space
hopping off soft ledges

steady skips one miss
Turkish rug flopped
on the fireplace brick
hitched under
flashlight and tippy-toe
under the blanket's night

Bats

rats, the bats are out / chittering and chirping / the sound
my gold necklace makes / when i set it in its place / among
my other pieces / in the Korean jewelry box / my ex gave me

i wondered if bats / like penguins / mate monogamously

so i read that they give oral / have sex in the air sometimes /
the male is a whore

and just like our moms / bat moms / are iconic / a single
nipple can carry the weight of her baby / who hangs on with
its / baby claw-toes latched on to her underside / as she
flies and carries / the weight of the goddamn world

get in the stroller

Earth
we all lay atop
her postpartum belly
the wind her reaching arms
the clouds her thoughts
/ weeping cries
bend the knees of our big hearts
children, she says
time cannot denote
her antiquity

life, an experiment

Pandora is a chemist
she mixes two atoms in her imagination
and forgives us for hating life
like looking into two mirrors
an endless hug of beings
unfortunate as it seems
this world's ugliness is our meaning

from unconditional love we are born
into a time-encapsulated rocket
the one variable that changes
as often as we do:
time

looking into murky waters
little creatures dart and flee
the eyes of a being from one hundred lives ago
scarier than the depths of dark nooks and crannies

inertia, a fall fragrant fog
theorizing and testing

what outcome does she desire
pain, the sharp flashes of a minnow's body

like thoughts, bubbles pop up to the surface

follow the flowing current

The Little Beauties

vase on a wooden table, a lace doily underneath, a single red rose drooping ever so slightly toward the window, as if to peer out onto the bustling street and river to view the miniature stories unlocked in the shadow box of its glass life

the books on the shelves pushed to varying sides like a woman pretends not to care while caring so deeply in her thoughtful poise and steps she caresses her cheek, rubs her neck, crosses her feet, while observing the deep varying colors in your eyes she thinks, *such beauty*

ode to my daughter

capture an image

a piece of the now past

a moment

i was sitting on the couch

a brown pleather 3-seater

at the end where i can see a portion of my room

one bay window and the square of sunlight leaning in over

the beige carpet

i see you run

just a snapshot of the full run from wall to wall

because you stop in the sunlight just right in my line of sight

and you spin in a slow inquisitive circle

in that light you stop and look at me

you smile and run off out of sight

your short curly hair bouncing

your small stature wearing white bloomers

this moment was so fleeting

i knew it was already a sentimental memory

Babe Babbles

for my daughter

lips straight as the horizon
hair like the redwoods
ember eyes licking the edges of cherrywood
hair as soft as down
skin like translucent polar fur
lashes long like the budding blades of lawn grass
eyes clear as eggshells
nails sharp like the edges of fern leaves
love pushed against my chest
the smell of silky sweet butter almonds and honey
a concoction of infinite love

Bubba

for my son

You smell adjacent to maple syrup or warm honey buttered biscuits, sweet like the warm inside of a monarch's cocoon. Your fabric soft and smooth with rough crevices from eczema. Your hair fine and obstinate in its curved waves. Your eyes dark yet so light as they observe, curiously absorbing the world. Your hands overturning mine again and again studying the lines and textures of me. The feeling is like effervescence when you smile at me: a high, clear bubble, liquifying colors up against the outline of the pale moon.

ethereal

purple turquoise green orange
bubbles
that look like floating letter e's
color the sunset sky over
nimbus clouds
and nebulous thoughts
your curly brown hair
creates an orange glow around your head
in the sunlight you pour more suds
squeal and jump
the wind blows the bubbles onto your brother and i
and they lightly pop on our skin
like cold sticky kisses
there's a magic to this sunset
with bubbles in the sky

Note from the Author

(For when times feel too difficult to keep going.)

Page from my diary September 11, 2023:

"Sometimes I feel I might just roll over and die from extreme exhaustion. The requirements to keep going, cleaning, working, walking, cooking, eating, and even sleeping, gripped by the force of burden. The sheer willpower I must muster from the depths of my body to not fall asleep right here, right now. This time in my life is shrouded in burden, the demands of children, society, my job. Yet, I miss this time already. The youth, the ableism, the growth, the love and interest my children shower over me. And how does one cope with so much change? So many demands? I feel like my progress has halted because I have slowed down. Yet everything continues to move."

This is a reminder that you are not alone. You can and will keep going. You must. I am here with you now, cheering you on, supporting you, seeing you, and encouraging your strength and bravery. Keep going. Even if all you did today was survive.

Acknowledgements

I'm eternally grateful for my children. I am so lucky to be their mom. Without them, I would not have written this book or understood half of the battles mothers face in the current political, economic, and social climate in which we live.

Joyce, mom, thank you for supporting me through my most difficult times in life. Without your encouragement, love, and your own maternal rage, this book would not have been possible. I've taken a lot of your energy and passion for change to heart in my efforts to make the world a better place.

Thank you to my friends, my pillars, my community: Taylor for always encouraging me, peer reviewing my work, and being so supportive through my divorce. Thank you for taking the leap on your own poetry and in your personal life. You have inspired me to do the same. Alyssa for being my right-hand businesswoman, event coordinator, and confidante. Thank you for always answering the phone, for sharing whine nights with me, and helping me realize my potential, worth, and value (and consistently reminding me when I've lost motivation). TJ for your love, kindness, and giving spirit as you helped pick me up, dust me off, and literally help me put my life back together. Thank you for caring for me and the kids. I don't even want to imagine what the first 6 months of single motherhood would have been like without your consistent emotional and physical support. Christie for mothering me through single motherhood, for talking me through the ups and downs of the daily chaos and mundaneness of motherhood, and for encouraging me the whole way. You are the spirit guide, single mom friend, and mentor I desperately needed leading up to the creation of this book.

There are so many others I have to thank. I could write a whole book to those of you that have helped me whether in big ways or just by being kind to me. Thank you.

About the Author

Raquel Medora is a Texas native. She received a BA in English from UT Austin with a Creative Writing Certificate in Poetry. Her publications include "Fireflies for Eyes" (2017) and "Gerber Daisy" (2019) in *Texas' Best Emerging Poets Series*. Her poem "I'm Beginning to Think There's No Such Thing as Extroverts" placed first in Pflugerville's annual Poetry Writing Contest (2021). Outside of writing, most of her time is spent raising her two young children, so her current hobbies include reading children's books, going on walks, and doing arts and crafts with her kids.

To see what Raquel is working on next follow her on Instagram **@raquel.medora** or visit her website **https://raquelmedorapoetry.com/**